The Legend of --

The Sheepskin

(A Special Gift of the Shepherds to the Christ Child)

by MIRIAM TAYLOR WERT
(in collaboration with daughter,
SUSAN WERT VOGT)

With love,
Susan W. Vogt

The Legend of The Sheepskin: A Special Gift of the Shepherds to the Christ Child

Trilogy Christian Publishers A Wholly Owned Subsidiary of Trinity Broadcasting Network

2442 Michelle Drive Tustin, CA 92780

Manufactured in the United States of America

10 9 8 7 6 5 4 3 2 1

Library of Congress Cataloging-in-Publication Data is available.

ISBN: 978-1-64773-404-6

E-ISBN: 978-1-64773-405-3

Dedication

I dedicate this book to the memory of my husband, **C. Marlin Wert,** who passed to be with Jesus on July 29, 2014, at the age of 91. He was a veteran of World War II, and he was a faithful and loving husband, father, grandfather and great-grandfather. He supported me one hundred percent through our seventy years of marriage.

I also dedicate this book to the memory my daughter, Peggy Wert Love, who passed to be with Jesus in September of 2015, at the age of 68. And to her husband, Norman F. Love, for being a faithful and loving husband, father, grandfather, and son-in-law.

My love and appreciation for my late son-in-law, Harold D. Vogt, and daughter Sue, who prepared accommodations in 2015 for me to spend my last years at their home beginning the fall of 2016.

--Miriam Taylor Wert
1/17/1925--12/18/2019

Acknowledgements

With a grateful heart, I wish to acknowledge the help and inspiration that my daughter, Susan Wert Vogt, has given me while writing my books. As she read my original manuscript of *The Sheepskin* (now Part 1 which ended with the Christmas story), she had a vision of how the gift of the sheepskin could be used for me to write new, additional chapters to include New Testament accounts of Jesus' ministry here on earth, up to His ascension to heaven.

After Sue shared these with me and I sat at my computer, I felt inspired as to how to weave them into my story – not only to add to it concerning the shepherds, but also how to glorify my Savior!

Susan is also a published author, and her expertise has been of utmost value in helping me not only in this endeavor, but in opening her home to me in 2016, where I went to reside at the age of 91.

Table of Contents

Preface

May your life be enriched as you read this story based on the biblical truths of Christianity. The shepherds were a part of the Christmas story, but the characters below are fictional.

Go with Abner ben Ezra,* the senior shepherd, as he meets the younger shepherds who have gathered with their flocks to join Abner in their annual trek to the special mountain pastures.

(*Note: It was an ancient tradition to use the term "ben" as a middle name to identify whose son the man or boy was. So, in the following account, ABNER ben EZRA is actually ABNER son of EZRA.)

The Sheepskin gives you a new perspective on the birth of Jesus Christ as seen through the eyes of lowly shepherds who receive the announcement of His birth and travel to Bethlehem to take a special gift of a sheepskin to the baby Jesus. Little did one of the younger shepherds realize how his life was to be affected in later years by this gift. No longer are these men just "the shepherds"– they are real, live men whom you know by name. Imagine yourself in their place. Let your imagination soar!

But this isn't a story just about the shepherds and the birth of the Savior. It also includes the life, death, and resurrection of Jesus Christ as it might have been told to this youngest shepherd concerning Christ's life on earth, His promise of the coming of the Holy Spirit, and the accounts of His ascension.

Much of the truth of the Christmas story comes to us in the Bible in the Gospel of Luke. Angels appeared to the shepherds who were led by a star to Bethlehem. The fictional dialogues of the shepherds are not meant to take away from, nor add to, the biblical account. Instead, the intention is to "bring alive" the shepherds as real people, as you read of their experiences and sense their thrill and excitement!

The important message is that Christ was born in Bethlehem, of a mother who was a virgin, as foretold by the prophets of God centuries before. Shepherds did have the experience of hearing and seeing the angel and the heavenly host, and they were able to testify orally to others then, as well as to all believers down through the ages by the written Word.

Note: It is important to keep in mind the scripture references in this story as shown here are in *italics*. By including the scripture in the conversations of the shepherds, the real message is conveyed. The scripture is of the utmost importance in conjunction with the conversations of the shepherds. It is not meant to take away from the sacredness or authenticity of the biblical account. When the story characters simply refer to a scripture verse but don't quote it directly, the words are not in italics, but the scripture reference is still given so the reader may verify.

Chapter 1
The Senior Shepherd

"Ah, Maria," Abner ben Ezra said to his wife one morning about 2,000 years ago, "I am not so sure I can make this journey to the far-away hills again this year." After pausing and giving a big sigh, Abner continued as if speaking his thoughts, "Oh, I may."

"Dear husband Abner," Maria replied, "I know you get tired more easily, and I am sorry it is necessary for you to continue to stay up in the hills with our flock of sheep. But then, the wool and the meat from our sheep are our only sources of income. I wish I could do something to make it easier for you. Couldn't you keep our flock here on the plain instead of going into the hills?"

"But, dear wife, as I have told you before, there are now so many flocks on the surrounding plains that pasture has become quite scarce. There is enough grass only for those shepherds who grow the sheep for sacrifices at the Holy Temple. We are willing to pasture our flocks some distance from home so the sacrificial lambs may be pastured where they are easily available to the Temple."

Abner continued, "I know that Jehovah God impressed on me the other year to go to the Judean hills and then over to the southwest side where the grass grows well this time of year. And an added blessing is the stream that tumbles down the slope but gathers at level spots in quiet pools for our flocks. Our flock and the small flocks of those with whom I shared this discovery are the only ones who go to that secluded area. Without God having led me there, I do believe we could not continue to keep our flock."

"Yes, praise Jehovah for His leading," Maria replied, "but I must admit that sometimes I wonder if it was

His will for you to share that area with the six young shepherds? It occurs to me that this may be one of the reasons you don't look forward to returning each year. Or do you think it is because you tire more easily than you once did?"

"My wife, how well you know me," replied Abner, "yes, I am older and more tired, but it's more than that. As the oldest shepherd in the group, I find that those who are younger make fun of me behind my back. Why, as we came down from the hills last year, I overheard Josiah say to Ethan, 'Just look at old Abner–I don't see how his old legs can carry him next year, or how he will have the strength to stay if he does make it.'

"Now I ask you, dear wife, do I really look that old and frail? Could it be that I would be wise to pay a younger man to take my place to shepherd our small flock? But then, I don't see how we could afford to do that."

"Dear husband," replied Maria, "I believe you are allowing another to do your thinking for you! No, you do not look old and frail. True, you may not show the strength and vitality of your youth, but then neither do I! The one thing that can help keep you in good health and allow you to live yet many years is to go on as you always have; but you must be wise to rest when necessary and then to travel at your own speed."

Continuing, she stated, "When you get there, be sure your shelter is in good condition to protect you on the cool nights as you watch the sheep. Also, gather an extra large pile of grass to make your bed pallet more comfortable for your aching bones when you can relax a little in the daytime. When you feel you need some extra rest, don't be ashamed to ask one of the young men to include our small flock under his watchful eye, even as he watches his own."

"Yes, yes, Maria," Abner replied a little impatiently, "but there is more to this than you understand. You see, many times I make suggestions or want to help those young shepherds, but they don't want to hear anything from me. I could be of so much help to them because of my many years of experience. You would think they might respect me as the elder shepherd but, instead, they seem to resent me and to turn a deaf ear. Often, they make mistakes because they are careless and lackadaisical and don't pay attention to the sheep under their care. Of course, they don't like it when I remind them this would not have happened if they had taken my advice."

"I see," Maria said thoughtfully, "perhaps it is your attitude with them that isn't quite right, Abner. You know, younger people like to think for themselves and to try things their way. When they make mistakes after you have tried to advise them, do you think it may be better to lend them a sympathetic ear instead of giving them the idea of 'I told you so?'"

"But how would I be helping them by doing that?," asked Abner. "They will never be better shepherds if I don't share with them what I have learned over the years. They will continue to see their lambs and sheep get sick and die from lack of care. I can stand it if they don't seem to care for me because I am older, but I can't sit by and see the animals suffer–I love animals too much to let that happen."

"Of course you do, Abner," Maria answered sympathetically, "but sometimes we just have to do our very best and let that be an example to the younger ones. When they see that you succeed and your sheep are stronger and kept safer than theirs, perhaps they will learn from you in that way. Most of all, it is important for you to show them that you love them as if they were the sons we have never had, and that you genuinely care about them and their animals."

Upon hearing no reply from Abner, Maria continued, "Yes, dear husband, they should respect you as their elder, but it is important that you respect them and admire their youthful vigor. Perhaps you could pay them a compliment when they really do something right. Who knows, it might even be contagious; and you may find they admire some of your traits also! If they sense your love and care, they will be more likely to seek your advice at a time when needed."

As they finished breakfast, Abner turned to his wife of many years. "Ah, Maria, as so often it has been, your advice is wise and it encourages me. I shall try to follow your suggestions, and I pray that I may set a good example for my younger friends. I go now to lead my flock to the foot of the Judean hills where I shall meet with the young shepherds to make our way to the pastures over the high hills. I shall miss you and our little home; and already I look forward to seeing you again at the end of this grazing season. Good-bye until then."

"Good-bye, dear husband," replied Maria, "I shall miss having you here, but I will keep busy weaving good heavy-weight woolen clothing for you for winter, as well as light-weight things for spring. Thanks to your faithfulness in caring for our sheep, we are blessed to have our own wool so I may make clothing. I shall be praying for you as I work."

Abner took the lead reins of his faithful old donkey, loaded with dried meats, figs, dates, olives, and tea leaves, as well as lentils and dried vegetables for making soup, and the cooking pot and other supplies needed for his stay in the hills. He picked up his shepherd's rod, staff, and slingshot and started to lead his flock toward his meeting with the young shepherds.

Chapter 2
The Younger Shepherds

As Abner and his flock reached the foot of the hills, he saw waiting for him Josiah ben Amon, Aaron ben Zaduk, Asa ben Immer, Jacob ben Shuham, Jorah ben Joab, and Ethan ben Guni. Each had a donkey to carry his supplies, and his flock of sheep was gathered around him. As Abner drew near to the young men, he breathed this quiet prayer:

"Lord God, Jehovah, give me real love and respect for these young men. Allow me to be an example to them without being judgmental and critical when they make mistakes. And, if it isn't asking too much, may I feel their love and respect in return so we may learn much from each other."

"Greetings, Abner," Josiah called out as Abner approached, "we were not sure you would be with us this year, but we are glad to see you could make it."

Remembering that it had been Josiah who had talked behind his back on the way home the previous year, at first, Abner felt this may have been a sarcastic remark. But then God impressed on him that Josiah was genuinely glad to see him.

Abner replied, "Yes, Josiah, and I am most happy and thankful to be able to make it again this year. Perhaps you and the others will understand it if I take more time than you do to get up the hills. It seems to be a little harder each year to make it on these old legs."

"Why, Abner," chimed in Aaron, "we often think how great it is that you have the strength to do as well as you do. We hope we can get along that well when we reach your age."

"Yes, Abner," added Asa, "you can be sure that one of us will rest with you along the way as you find you must stop for a time, until you are able to start out again. You see, we need you to be with us during the long nights, especially while we watch our flocks."

"Well now boys, that sure is good of you, and I thank you," Abner said brightly. "I had been thinking I was nothing but a burden to you younger ones. Just from your encouraging words, I find strength returning to my body and my spirit."

A short distance away, Ethan turned to Jacob and said quietly, "Well, I'm not too happy about being delayed by this old man. Maybe the rest of you want to lose time, but I don't. Don't count me in as one to stay behind with him. I'm anxious to get to the pasture land and get my sheep settled before night falls."

Upon overhearing Ethan's remark to Jacob, Jorah commented, "Well, Ethan, in a way I feel like you do. I don't know whether or not I will wait with him either, and yet I do feel we should give him a chance."

As they started on their way, Abner seemed to be quite strong but, after a time, several of his younger sheep tried to stray away from his flock, and he had to go after them to bring them back. Each time this happened, he became more tired.

Several times, the elder shepherd found it necessary to slow down and then to rest, and the younger men took turns stopping with him and keeping watch over Abner's flock along with their own. By helping in this way, all of them were able to get up into the hills and just over the brow to the good pasture land before dark.

Of course, Ethan had reached the place first and had claimed the choicest spot. Soon, he was joined by Jorah who had stopped only once to wait rather impatiently with Abner. But finally, all of them arrived with their sheep.

They were overjoyed to see that the stream of water was still abundant. Each was able to place his flock in a position where it would not be far from where the stream reached a somewhat flat "bench" on the hill and the flow of water collected in a placid pool. There, the sheep could drink without fear and the shepherds could refresh themselves during the warmer part of the upcoming days.

From the previous years, they knew they could work their way down the hill as days went by to find a new pasture area after the sheep cropped the grass. A series of those flat "benches" in the contour of the hill allowed peaceful pools of water to form as they made their descent. This meant the shepherds and their flocks could move down to lower areas and still have water.

By the time they needed to move back up to better pasture, the grass would be replenished again at the top of the hill, and they could take the sheep up there and work their way down again if necessary. Abner never ceased to give thanks to God for having led him to this perfect grazing area some years before.

Abner kept a watchful eye on his flock each night, never allowing himself to drift off to sleep or to lessen his attention to them. He knew there were predators in the area that could attack and kill his sheep, and he was determined to be a watchful caretaker so that would not happen.

Night after night, Abner found it necessary to call out to one of the six young shepherds, "Say there, wake up! Your flock is about to be attacked!"

As the young man awoke with a start, sometimes he would defend himself to Abner by making a remark about "a nosy old man". When this happened, Abner kept silent, recognizing that the young man was on the defensive because he knew he had done wrong by falling asleep. Instead of answering back in a defensive manner,

Abner wisely held his tongue and prayed silently that it may have been a good lesson for the young shepherd.

Ethan was the most defensive one, and he made it quite clear he didn't want to receive any advice or help from Abner. One night, Ethan said rather hotly to Abner, "I wish you would mind your own business. I know what I'm doing, and I don't need you to keep me awake, old man!"

Chapter 3
A Glorious Night

One other night, as Abner remained watchful while the younger shepherds were in a state between dozing and being awake, without warning, a great light shone on them! The angel of the Lord appeared in the light. Amazed and awestruck, Abner cried out to the young shepherds to awaken. As they did, they were terrified at this strange sight.

But the angel said to them, "Do not be afraid. I bring you good news of great joy that will be for all people. Today in the town of David a Savior has been born to you; he is Christ the Lord. This will be a sign to you: You will find a baby wrapped in cloths and lying in a manger."

Suddenly a great company of the heavenly host

appeared with the angel, praising God and saying, "Glory to God in the highest, and on earth peace to men on whom his favor rests." When the angels had left them and gone into heaven, the shepherds said to one another, "Let's go to Bethlehem and see this thing that has happened, which the Lord has told us about" (Luke 2: 10-15).

But before they felt they could start, the younger shepherds turned to Abner, all talking at once: "Did the angel mean Bethlehem when he said the town of David? Can we go to see him right away?"

As Abner replied that Bethlehem was indeed the place described by the angel, the younger shepherds wanted to leave immediately. But one of them was missing!

Earlier, Ethan had neglected to watch his sheep. The

flock had been scattered down across the hill, and Ethan had to go in search of them. Although he saw the great light and heard voices, Ethan couldn't make his way back in time to go with the other young shepherds.

Abner said to the other five, "You men go back down into the plains from which we came, and then on to Bethlehem. My slow travel would hold you back too much, and I know you want to get there quickly. May God give you a real blessing as you go on this great mission. I shall pray for you as you go, and I shall keep watch over your flocks as best I can, with God's help."

They wanted to leave quickly, but they had more questions. They asked Abner how they could be sure this was really a message from God and that they were not just dreaming. Abner assured them this birth had been foretold by their Jewish prophet, Micah, who had said it would be in Bethlehem (Micah 5:2-5a).

Next, they wondered how they would find the stable where the baby was in the manger. Abner told them to go back to the top of the hill behind them where he felt there would be some sign for them to follow as they started down the other side. And so the younger shepherds went, and it was from the hilltop they first saw the star shining down upon Bethlehem. By keeping sight of its unusually distinct rays, they were able to continue their journey unerringly.

* * *

In the meantime, soon after the others left, Ethan came back with his flock of sheep he had rescued. He asked Abner about the light and the voices he had heard, and he wondered where the other shepherds were. Abner told him with great excitement how they had been visited by the angel of the Lord and of the message they had received!

Although Ethan was excited, he was also sick at heart to think he had missed being present for such a glorious occasion. He told Abner he was sorry he had not listened to his advice about taking care of his sheep.

* * *

A Gift for the Christ Child

Upon seeing Ethan's sincere remorse, Abner said, "Take heart, Ethan, for I do believe you have time to catch the others if you hurry and call loudly to them as you go. And oh yes, in the excitement we forgot about their taking a gift to the newborn babe. I would have liked to have sent a young lamb, but we have none of an age to leave its mother.

"But, here, I have a new sheepskin all wrapped and clean, as Maria had packed an extra one for me for cool nights and I have never used it. Take it as a gift from all of us to the baby, but do run now. I shall watch your flock."

Looking into Abner's eyes with great appreciation and love, Ethan thanked him for giving him the honor of taking the gift and for making it possible for him to go with the other shepherds. After a time, Ethan caught up with the others and told them Abner had sent a gift for them to give to the baby. They all rejoiced and gave thanks to Jehovah for this wise, older shepherd who had done so much for them.

So they hurried off and found Mary and Joseph, and the baby, who was lying in the manger (Luke 2:16).

As they went into Bethlehem, there was no mistaking the exact stable upon which the star was shining! Humbly, they presented the gift of the sheepskin to Mary, telling her how Abner had given it to them to give as a gift to the baby. As Mary gratefully accepted the sheepskin, she smiled and laid it gently over the manger where the baby was sleeping.

When they had seen him, they spread the word concerning what had been told them about this child, and all who heard it were amazed at what the shepherds said to them (Luke 2:17).

* * *

Meanwhile, Abner was meditating on all that had taken place. He was impressed with the fact that the angels' appearance in the great light was a very local thing, possibly seen only by him and the young shepherds because of their location on the back (southwest) side of the large hill. There had been no sign of the light or the angels prior to their sudden appearance above them, not very high in the sky.

Other shepherds on the northeast side of the hill,

up which he had brought his sheep, would not have been able to see the angels or the light; and so it was quite possible that his group was the only one so blessed that night.

Chapter 4
Age Barrier Is Gone

About noon of the second day, Abner heard the young shepherds talking excitedly to each other as they came over the hill. As they reached Abner, words came tumbling out of them in a torrent as they told how they had been guided by the star, what they had seen, how they had given the gift to the beautiful, young mother, and how they had gone throughout the town and countryside telling everyone what they had seen.

As they told him everything, Abner felt as if he had lived through the experience with them, and he was most blessed and thankful. He told them how he had been able to sit and pray for them, meditate on God's goodness and rejoice that God had given to them first the news of the birth of their Messiah.

With great humility, Abner shared with them how

he had searched the Jewish scriptures all his adult life and had longed to see the fulfillment of the prophecy given there about the birth of the coming Messiah. And now, it had come to pass, and they had been blessed to hear the great news from God by way of the angels!

The younger shepherds admitted they had not studied the scriptures and did not remember that their elders had spoken of the great promise, and so they hadn't known about it. They thanked Abner from the bottom of their hearts for sharing with them about the fulfillment of the prophecies, and for making it possible for them to see that fulfillment. They also agreed they wanted to know more about the Jewish scriptures and so they asked Abner to teach them as he could find time to do so. Abner said he would be most grateful to do just that.

The next day, Abner said, "Jorah, would you go down into the valley to tell the good news to Maria and the relatives and friends of all of us? We will watch over your flock until you return." Jorah replied that he was privileged to be the bearer of such good news. "By the way," Abner added, "be sure to tell Maria that I sent her sheepskin as a gift to the baby so that now she may want to send me another one."

Thus it was that Ethan and Jorah, who at times had resented Abner, were blessed by him on this great occasion. Abner was thankful that his change of heart and attitude had helped him to really see inside the hearts of all these men. He had learned that he needed to love them even as God did—unconditionally. Life would never be the same for any of them because now they knew their Messiah had come!

* * *

News about the Sheepskin

As Jorah made his way down the hillside to the valley

below, the young shepherd was filled with gladness because of the good news he carried to share with friends and loved ones. In fact, he planned to share it with every person he met along the way, just as he and the other shepherds had done the night of Christ's birth. Oh, what joy filled his heart!

But, as his thoughts went back over that blessed night, one thing kept coming into his mind to cast some shadow on an otherwise perfect event. He had been so excited, along with the other shepherds, that he had failed to mention it to them as they made their way back to Abner and their sheep.

Jorah didn't know much about the Jewish scriptures, that was true, but from long ago he recalled having heard adults tell of how any offering or sacrifice made to God had to be spotless and perfect. A lamb or a dove had to be healthy and as near as possible to being perfect when it was taken to be sacrificed to God.

Jorah thought to himself, "Then, shouldn't any gift given to Christ the Lord have been perfect also? I'm sure this should be, and so I wonder about what I saw. The sheepskin gift was still folded with care just as it had been when Maria placed it in the woven bag for Abner to take along to the hills. It looked perfect when it was removed from the bag and handed to the baby's mother.

"But how well I remember the shock I felt when I saw Mary unfolding the sheepskin to place over the manger. On the very last fold, just as the one corner was draped down over the manger, I saw that the entire corner was marked with a distinct stain of dark red. I shall never forget that sight," Jorah recalled.

"The mother either didn't see the mark," he further reasoned, "or she was too gracious to show she had. I know she was thankful for the sheepskin and would not have wanted to embarrass anyone by showing any surprise. But now I wonder . . . ?"

Jorah stopped pondering those thoughts, however, as he reached the valley and started meeting people. Nothing could interfere with his telling them of that wonderful night of the birth of the Christ Child, their Messiah:

1. How it had been announced to him and the shepherds with him;

2. Their asking Abner if this really could be true and his assurance that it was;

3. How they had been guided by a great star to find the stable;

4. Their walking/running to get to the manger;

5. The unforgettable first sight of the Christ Child;

6. Their presenting him with his first gift. How excited Jorah became as he relived the event each time he told it!

Jorah's final stop was to see Abner's wife, Maria. She was thrilled as Jorah told of the eventful night. But when he started to tell how Abner had sent his unused sheepskin as a gift for the baby, Maria's mouth opened in shocked surprise. "Oh, no," Maria exclaimed, "it should not have been that one!"

Seeing the surprise on Jorah's face at her exclamation, Maria said, "You see, I had just finished drying the sheepskin one day and laid it on the table where I was dying wool to use in making some clothes for myself. I had made dye from some berries, as I always do. I was not as careful as I should have been and some of the hot dye splashed onto the edge of the sheepskin. I had no time to prepare another skin for Abner to take with him, and so I wrapped it in the woven bag as soon as it was dry and said nothing about the stain. I knew–or at least I thought then–that Abner would be the only one to see the mark and that it wouldn't bother him for he would be using it only in the hills. Oh, why, why wasn't I more careful? The gift for the Christ Child should have been perfect."

Jorah expressed his sympathy for Maria and said he felt sure Abner would understand. Even though Jorah didn't know much about God, he told Maria he felt sure God had known it was a gift from the heart and so would not hold its imperfection against Abner or Maria. Somehow, Jorah was not as fearful of God as he had been, for he had seen God's Son, the Christ Child. Now Jorah felt God's love and knew his heart would never be the same.

Maria found another sheepskin to send to Abner, even though it wasn't a new one, and packed it and some more provisions for Abner before giving them to Jorah. He wanted to get back to the hills as quickly as he could, because he knew the others were doing extra work to take care of his flock in addition to their own.

When he reached the grazing area, Jorah was hesitant about telling Abner and the others of the stained sheepskin but realized he must do so without delay. When he told the story about seeing the stain, Jorah was amazed to learn that Ethan had also seen it but had said nothing. Abner reassured them that God would understand because it hadn't been intentional on anyone's part to give an imperfect gift. Abner said, "I believe God looks on the heart at such times and understands."

* * *

The remaining months in the hills passed rather uneventfully for the shepherds in comparison with the great event they had shared together. There was a new relationship of love and concern for each other as they learned to pray together. They enjoyed those times

43

when Abner taught them about the spiritual history of their people and also about the prophecies that had been fulfilled and were yet to be fulfilled. Little did they know, one of them would be a witness to some of the fulfillments.

As the shepherds came down into the valley after months of the grazing season in the hills, they went their separate ways to their homes with the promise of getting together the next season for a return trip. This time no words were said behind Abner's back. All of the younger shepherds embraced the older man, and he embraced them in return. Now, a special bond existed among young and old that would never be broken on this earth.

Part 2

(in collaboration with daughter, Susan Wert Vogt)

Chapter 5

The Fulfillment of Scriptures through the Christ Child

When they met together the next season to return to the hills, Jorah had a startling tale for them: "You know, about a month after I returned home last year," Jorah told them, "I had an amazing experience. I had reason to be in the western part of our country, along the road that leads down into Egypt."

He continued, "Coming towards me was a man leading a donkey on which a woman was sitting, holding a small child. Just as they passed where I was standing, I saw that the woman was sitting on a sheepskin on the back of the donkey. I could hardly keep from crying out when I saw the red stain on a corner of the sheepskin.

"Yes, it was the mother holding the Christ Child, and she was made more comfortable by using the very gift we had given her the night of his birth! They seemed to be in a hurry for some reason, and so I didn't try to stop them although I surely would have liked to have spoken with them. Later, I inquired of some friends I have in Jerusalem, and also some in Bethlehem, in an attempt to discover what may have occurred," Jorah continued, "and here is what was on record:"

After Jesus was born in Bethlehem in Judea, during the time of King Herod, Magi from the east came to Jerusalem and asked, "Where is the one who has been born king of the Jews? We saw his star in the east and have come to worship him" (Matthew 2:1-2).

"Just think," Asa said in awe, as he interrupted Jorah, "that must have been the very same star that led us to the stable earlier! It just makes me realize even more how greatly God blessed us on that special night." All of the shepherds nodded in agreement.

"This is the rest of what was on record," continued Jorah:

When King Herod heard this, he was disturbed and all Jerusalem with him. When he had called together all the people's chief priests and teachers of the law, he asked them where the Christ was to be born. "In Bethlehem in Judea," they replied, "for this is what the prophet has written 'But you, Bethlehem, in the land of Judah, are by no means least among the rulers of Judah; for out of you will come a ruler who will be the shepherd of my people Israel."

Then Herod called the Magi secretly and found out from them the exact time the star had appeared. He sent them to Bethlehem and said, "Go and make a careful search for the child. As soon as you find him, report to me, so that I too may go and worship him."

After they had heard the king, they went on their way, and the star they had seen in the east went ahead of them until it stopped over the place where the child was. When they saw the star, they were overjoyed. On coming to the house, they saw the child with his mother, Mary, and they bowed down and worshipped him. Then they opened their treasures and presented him with gifts of gold and of incense and of myrrh. And having been warned in a dream not to go back to Herod, they returned to their country by another route.

When they had gone, an angel of the Lord appeared to Joseph in a dream. "Get up," he said, "take the child and his mother and escape to

Egypt. Stay there until I tell you, for Herod is going to search for the child to kill him."

So he got up, took the child and his mother during the night and left for Egypt (Matthew 2:3-14).

"And to think," Jorah said, "I was so blessed to be standing by the road as the little family went through on their way down to Egypt! I know they got away safely from Herod because no one was following them, and they would have been on the way for many hours by that time! In fact, it could have been the second day. Anyhow, it's good they were far away from Bethlehem by then, because this is what happened after they left":

When Herod realized that he had been outwitted by the Magi, he was furious, and he gave orders to kill all the boys in Bethlehem and its vicinity who were two years old and under, in accordance with the time he had learned from the Magi (Matthew 2:16).

"Can you imagine any king acting like that!?" exclaimed Aaron. "I think anyone would love the child we saw and any other little babies or children instead of wanting to kill them! How will all this fit into God's plan now?" The listening men showed their concern over this same question, praying in their hearts that the Christ child would be kept safe. Abner led them all in praise to God for His mercy and goodness.

* * *

As they continued to discuss this latest information, Josiah also told them he had received information from a friend in Nazareth, filling the gaps in the part of the story they had not known about the Christ child:

In the sixth month, God sent the angel Gabriel to

Nazareth, a town in Galilee, to a virgin pledged to be married to a man named Joseph, a descendant of David. The virgin's name was Mary. The angel went to her and said, "Greetings, you who are highly favored! The Lord is with you."

Mary was greatly troubled at his words and wondered what kind of greeting this might be. But the angel said to her, "Do not be afraid, Mary, you have found favor with God. You will be with child and give birth to a son, and you are to give him the name Jesus. He will be great and will be called the Son of the Most High. The Lord God will give him the throne of his father David, and he will reign over the house of Jacob forever; his kingdom will never end."

"How will this be," Mary asked the angel, "since I am a virgin?"

The angel answered, "The Holy Spirit will come

upon you, and the power of the Most High will overshadow you. So the holy one to be born will be called the Son of God (Luke 1:26, 29, 34-35).

Asa spoke up immediately, "So *that* explains how a virgin gave birth to the Christ child and why his name is Jesus! I was wondering about that and about the name of Joseph in the story about the Magi. Now we know that Joseph was Mary's betrothed husband, and he was taking care of Mary and Jesus." The other shepherds admitted that it cleared their thinking on the matter also, and they were thankful for the information and this further proof that Jesus was the Son of God.

* * *

More News of the Christ Child

The next year when the shepherds went together into the hills, Jacob told them he had received good news from his uncle in Nazareth that Jesus had been returned safely from Egypt and was living with Joseph and Mary in the small town of Nazareth:

And the child grew and became strong; he was filled with wisdom, and the grace of God was upon him (Luke 2:40).

All of them expressed thankfulness to God for the safe return of this child who had come to mean so much to them.

There was much discussion among the shepherds during that grazing season because they knew it was to be their last one together. Abner had told them he would not be able to return again, which was sad news to the younger men. So it was that they bid each other their last good-byes that year, with all of them expressing the hope they would see each other again.

The younger shepherds knew they had some decisions of their own to make since some of their own fathers were getting older. Traditionally, the family inheritance (land, sheep, etc.) was passed on to the eldest son in each family, so the younger sons could move on in their lives via other vocations if they were inclined.

* * *

Some months later, word was sent around to the group that their senior shepherd, Abner, had died in his sleep about a month after they came down from the hills. Although saddened to hear this, all of them were thankful he had been home with Maria when the time came for his soul to go to be with their God, about whom Abner had taught them so much.

Chapter 6
A New Beginning: "The Sons of Thunder"

There was no doubt in Ethan's mind as to what he wanted to do for he had often thought of the sea and of learning the fishing trade. He knew that his younger brother wanted to tend their father's flock and so Ethan's help would no longer be needed.

Ethan had started as a shepherd when he was young, and now he was free to form his plans in his mind and heart for the future. He stayed with his parents for about a year, during which time he received the word of Abner's death and was able to overcome his grief to a great extent.

Then Ethan said good-bye to his parents and, with their blessing, he headed for the Sea of Galilee to see if he would like the trade of his Uncle Zebedee, a very successful fisherman. Ethan looked forward to seeing his younger cousins, James and John, having heard so much about them down through the years.

When Ethan stopped to see his uncle, Zebedee agreed that he and his sons would train Ethan, during which time he would be given his room and board as pay. After his proven training, in addition he would be given a small wage. Ethan agreed to this offer, thinking it was most fair as his needs were not many.

Ethan found life to be anything but dull, living and working with these Sons of Thunder, as they were called. It was just a nickname given to them because they were loud and boisterous at times, but Ethan found this to be most welcome after the quiet life of a shepherd. He thrived on excitement.

Soon, he learned to become a good sailor and fisherman and was quite happy. Occasionally, Ethan recalled the experience of that wonderful night when he and the other shepherds visited the Christ child. He wondered where Jesus was now. After a year or so, Ethan felt comfortable enough with James and John to ask if they had heard of any one by that name.

The only information John could give him was what he had heard from a friend in Nazareth quite a number of years before. A twelve-year-old boy named Jesus had caused some grief to his parents when they found he was not in their company as they were returning home after taking part in the Feast of the Passover in Jerusalem.

They went back to Jerusalem to look for Jesus and were amazed to find him in the temple courts, sitting among the teachers, listening to them and asking them questions. His mother told him they had been anxiously searching for him, and Jesus asked them if they didn't know he had to be in his Father's house (Luke 2:41-49).

"You know," John said, "in addition to how impressed

my friend was with the boy's comments, he told me he had noticed something special about the mother. She had been riding on a donkey when she discovered the sheepskin had slipped off the donkey's back one time, she got off him. She wouldn't leave that site until she found it. Nobody could imagine why the sheepskin was so important to her since it had a red blemish on one of the corners."

"Of course," Ethan exclaimed, "that sheepskin was the gift we carried to the Christ child on the night of his birth!" Then, with great excitement, he told James and John the story of that night that would have taken place when James and John were very young children, perhaps even babies. He wondered if they believed he had been there that night.

The two cousins verified they had heard down through the years that shepherds had told of the angels and the birth of the Christ child. Ethan felt blessed to realize that Mary still had the sheepskin, and he was thankful that she still cherished this simple gift, even though later she had received more expensive gifts from the Magi.

* * *

Another year passed before Ethan was to hear more about Jesus. One day, as they were in the boat preparing their nets, Ethan saw a man about the age of James and John approaching the boat. After the man spoke with James and John, they left with him immediately and didn't return.

After a number of days Ethan missed his cousins, and so he asked Zebedee about them. Zebedee said his sons had decided not to work for him any longer, and they wouldn't be returning to the boat. Ethan wondered how Zebedee would accept this situation since it was expected that eventually a son would take over his father's trade.

But Ethan reasoned to himself, "Possibly Zebedee would feel that he, Zebedee's nephew, had learned enough about fishing to be a replacement for his sons, James and John."

(As an aside, Zebedee had joked to Ethan that at first he had been surprised at the impetuousness of his sons, "Perhaps, instead of 'Sons of Thunder,' their impetuousness should be attributed to their status-seeking mother who would 'stop at nothing' to get her sons promoted in the world! One thing sure, she wants the best for those boys!" Zebedee exclaimed.)

* * *

Later, Zebedee told Ethan that James and John had become followers of Jesus, the man with whom they had chosen to follow. When he heard the name, "Jesus," Ethan was amazed! Could it be? Yes, it had to be! The man he had seen that day was the age Ethan would have expected

Jesus to be by now. It amazed him to know that his cousins were now followers of Jesus! However, Jesus was becoming well-known in Galilee.

Jesus (was going) throughout Galilee, teaching in their synagogues, preaching the good news of the kingdom, and healing every disease and sickness among the people. News about him spread all over Syria, and people brought to him all who were ill with various diseases, those suffering severe pain, the demon-possessed, those having seizures, and the paralyzed, and he healed them. Large crowds from Galilee, the Decapolis, Jerusalem, Judea and the region across the Jordan followed him (Matthew 4:23-25).

Some months passed with no sign of James and John, and Ethan continued to work for Zebedee even though his curiosity about Jesus knew no bounds. One day, James and John stopped by to let Zebedee know that they were well and were happy serving Jesus full-time. With great excitement, they related to Zebedee and Ethan some of the events that had already taken place in Jesus' ministry throughout the countryside.

Although James and John were anxious to get back to Jesus, they felt it was important to witness to their father and Ethan, and so they stayed long enough to relay stories of their experiences.

"Not long after we started to follow Jesus," James said, "He had drawn us aside to start what proved to be his favorite manner of giving us special teaching. Jesus had chosen twelve of us to be his special disciples."

Simon (whom he named Peter), his brother Andrew, James, John, Philip, Bartholomew,

Matthew, Thomas, James son of Alphaeus, Simon who was called the Zealot, Judas son of James, and Judas Iscariot (Luke 6:14-16).

James continued, "Jesus taught us about loving our enemies, not judging others, and other important truths. After he had finished teaching us, we witnessed a great miracle!"

When Jesus had finished saying all this in the hearing of the people, he entered Capernaum. There a centurion's servant, whom his master valued highly, was sick and about to die. The centurion heard of Jesus and sent some elders of the Jews to him, asking him to come and heal his servant. When they came to Jesus, they pleaded earnestly with him, "This man deserves to have you do this, because he loves our nation and has built our synagogue." So Jesus went with them.

He was not far from the house when the centurion sent friends to say to him: "Lord, don't trouble yourself, for I do not deserve to have you come under my roof. That is why I did not even consider myself worthy to come to you. But say the word, and my servant will be healed. For I myself am a man under authority, with soldiers under me. I tell this one, 'Go,' and he goes; and that one, 'Come,' and he comes. I say to my servant, 'Do this,' and he does it."

When Jesus heard this, he was amazed at him, and turning to the crowd following him, he said, "I tell you, I have not found such great faith even in Israel." Then the man who had been sent returned to the house and found the servant well (Luke 7:1-10).

Ethan was awestruck to hear this and other true stories from the lips of these two men who had been so blessed as to be with Jesus; but soon they had to leave to get back to Jesus, and Ethan and Zebedee had to get back to their work with the nets.

Chapter 7
Ethan Witnesses a Miracle

One day after his sons had related the amazing events to Zebedee, he said to Ethan, "We will be needing some supplies from Gadara, just off the east shore, and I am trusting you to get them for me. It is a rather slow time for fishing just now, and so you may have several days to take one of our boats to make the trip and pick up the supplies. You will need to go ashore there and engage some help to bring the supplies to the boat."

Ethan replied, "I shall be happy to take care of it for you and will do my best to get the supplies and get back here by the time the run of fish has gotten better." His happiness would have been even greater if he had known what was in store for him.

Two days later, Ethan set sail for the eastern shore of the Sea of Galilee to perform the task for Zebedee.

As he made ready to pull into the shoreline, to his amazement, he saw James and John manning another boat as it pulled in to that same shoreline. When they disembarked, he realized the others were Jesus and the rest of the disciples. They were met by a strange sight– one that Ethan knew he would never forget!

They sailed to the region of the Gerasenes (Gadarenes), which is across the lake from Galilee. When Jesus stepped ashore, he was met by a demon-possessed man from the town. For a long time this man had not worn clothes or lived in a house, but had lived in the tombs. When he saw Jesus, he cried out and fell at his feet, shouting at the top of his voice, "What do you want with me, Jesus, Son of the Most High God? I beg you, don't torture me!" For Jesus had commanded the evil spirit to come out of the man. Many times it had seized him, and though he was chained hand and foot and kept under guard, he had broken his chains and had been driven by the demon into solitary places.

Jesus asked him, "What is your name?"

"Legion," he replied, because many demons had gone into him. And they begged him repeatedly not to order them to go into the Abyss.

A large herd of pigs was feeding there on the hillside. The demons begged Jesus to let them go into them, and he gave them permission. When the demons came out of the man, they went into the pigs, and the herd rushed down the steep bank into the lake and was drowned.

When those tending the swine saw what had happened, they ran off and reported this in the *town and countryside, and the people went out to see what had happened. When they came to Jesus, they found the man from whom the demons had gone out, sitting at Jesus' feet, dressed and in his right mind; and they were afraid. Those who had seen it told the people how the demon-possessed man had been cured. Then all the people of the region of the Gerasenes asked Jesus to leave them because they were overcome with fear. So he got into the boat and left (Luke 8:26-39).*

After witnessing this miracle, it was difficult for Ethan to get on with business as usual, but he had promised Zebedee he would get the supplies to him as soon as possible. So he tucked away the memory of this special day in his mind and heart and went on his way, although his heart had followed in the other boat with

Jesus and the disciples. Of course, he shared the event with Zebedee when he returned with the supplies.

Chapter 8
Ethan's Great Decision

Although it was only about six months before John stopped again, it seemed like an eternity to Ethan. When Ethan asked about Jesus, John said the Jewish leaders were opposed to the teachings of Jesus, and trouble might be brewing. Ethan expressed an interest in meeting Jesus, and John urged him to join some of the groups of people who gathered around Jesus everywhere He went, teaching and healing the sick.

John told Ethan, "One thing that has impressed me is that Jesus teaches us disciples, as well as the other people, by way of parables.

"Parables!" exclaimed Ethan, "What are they?"

John replied, "A parable is a story used from everyday life to teach a specific spiritual or moral truth. It's a very effective way of teaching because it brings the truths down to the level of many uneducated people, and their hearts are touched by those truths."

"Maybe I could even understand that type of teaching," Ethan said.

"I truly believe you could," John agreed, "and you would be most welcome to be one of the many followers."

John told him of the time Jesus told Nicodemus,

For God so loved the world that he gave his one and only Son, that whoever believes in him shall not perish but have everlasting life (John 3:16).

With joy, John heard Ethan say, "I believe in Jesus, and I'm certain He is the Son of God!" The two said good-bye to each other, expressing the wish that they might meet soon again.

After John left, Ethan reached the decision that he no longer wanted to be a fisherman, and that he had a real desire to learn more about Jesus. He told Zebedee he was sorry, but he would be leaving in several weeks and Zebedee should look for someone else. Ethan expressed his thanks to Zebedee for having provided training and work for him when he was in need, but said he felt it was important for him to leave so he could also follow Jesus.

Zebedee placed his arms around Ethan in a fatherly embrace and told him he had become like a son to him, but he understood why Ethan wanted to leave. He also said something that made Ethan feel much better about leaving: "My sister has been after me to take her two young sons on as helpers on my boat, and this gives me a great opportunity to answer her request."

Before long, the time came when Zebedee's nephews arrived, and Ethan was free to leave. He was excited as he left to follow Jesus. At first, he was content just to sit on the outer fringes of the crowd, but sometimes he had an intense desire to get in closer so he would not miss any of Christ's teachings. Ethan was especially thrilled one day to hear Jesus telling the Parable of the Lost Sheep, as it stirred memories of the past.

Then Jesus told them this parable: "Suppose one of you has a hundred sheep and loses one of them. Does he not leave the ninety-nine in the open country and go after the lost sheep until he finds it? And when he finds it, he joyfully puts it on his shoulders and goes home. Then he calls his friends and neighbors together and says, 'Rejoice with me; I have found my lost sheep.' I tell you that in the same way there will be more rejoicing in heaven over one sinner who repents than over ninety-nine righteous persons who do not need to repent" (Luke 15:3-7).

Ethan knew this was true from his own experiences as a shepherd, but it was good to hear Jesus teach the truth in this way, so that all could understand it. Jesus told a number of other parables, all of which contained great truths, but Ethan found the one about the lost sheep to be his favorite.

"Oh, if only I had decided sooner to follow Him," Ethan thought to himself many times as each day went by and his very soul was touched by the love flowing from Jesus into His disciples and all followers.

One day, Ethan told a new follower of Jesus, with intense excitement in his voice:

I shall never forget any of the events that I witnessed in connection with Jesus, but one stands out as what seemed then to be impossible; yes, it was a miracle! No doubt it seemed especially great simply because of its magnitude.

"I was in this great crowd of people—four thousand men, besides women and children—who had gathered to be with Jesus, to hear Him teach, and to witness the miracles of healing that were so natural with Him. We saw the mute speaking, the crippled made well, the lame walking and the blind seeing, and we praised the God of Israel.

"Jesus had compassion on the crowd, which had been with him for three days, and He reminded his disciples that this crowd had nothing to eat. He further told the disciples that he didn't want to send the people away hungry or they might collapse on the way.

"The disciples asked Jesus where they could get enough bread in that remote place to feed such a crowd. Then Jesus asked them how many loaves they had, and they told him they had seven, as well as a few small fish.

"I noticed this information about such a small

amount of food didn't seem to upset Jesus in the least. He just told the crowd to sit down on the ground. Then, he took the seven loaves and the fish, gave thanks, and broke them and gave them to the disciples, who then gave them to the people.

"Now, are you ready for this?" asked Ethan, wanting to emphasize what had occurred. "They all ate and were satisfied. Not only that, but afterward the disciples picked up seven basketfuls of broken pieces that were left over! (Matthew 15:29-39)

"I tell you, that was something to behold!" continued Ethan, "and John told me that Jesus had performed a similar miracle in another area when he had fed five thousand, plus women and children. After such evidence, how could anyone doubt that He was the Son of God? This is the kind of love and compassion constantly displayed by Jesus for people."

Chapter 9
Awesome Days

After one of the continuous weeks of travel on foot, Ethan felt especially footsore, weary, and upset in his stomach, leaving him weak. He decided to take a break from travel and find a place to rest along the way for several days. One of the men he had met in the group of followers had told him that a Christian believer had a room for rent on the outskirts of Jerusalem, and so Ethan stopped there for a few days until he could regain his strength.

By noon of the third day, Ethan was feeling better and had decided to try to locate Jesus and his followers, but something strange occurred! An unusual darkness came over the land, and it continued until three o'clock. Ethan wondered about the sudden darkness, but it seemed a good time to take a final rest. He awoke with a start at three o'clock, and a few minutes later the darkness had lifted completely.

Ethan decided to go into Jerusalem to find Jesus and the others. As he went, he noticed that some of the crowd he had usually seen with Jesus were walking toward him, and they were in tears. They told Ethan that Jesus had been crucified and where it had taken place! Ethan was crushed, but he knew he had to go on to find the place of crucifixion, to see for himself. But when he got there, he found that Jesus' body had already been removed from the cross and was gone. He saw a Roman centurion standing near the empty cross and, in anguish, he asked the centurion what had happened.

The centurion told him one thing he had noticed was that some women and a man were standing near the foot of the cross. The centurion had been told that one of the women was the mother of Jesus, who was on the cross, and that the man (John) was one of his disciples. He had heard Jesus saying something to them (John 19:25-27).

The centurion added, "Strange things took place here today. Darkness came over all the land from noon to three o'clock, then suddenly there was an earthquake when this Jesus cried out in a loud voice! We heard that the curtain of the temple was torn in two from top to bottom at that same time, and other unusual things took place in the city. The other guards and I were terrified by all of that, and I remember exclaiming,

Surely he was the Son of God! (Matthew 27:45, 50-54).

"Yes, surely he was the Son of God," agreed Ethan, "and now I know it was the earthquake that wakened me so suddenly at three o'clock today! Please, can you tell me anything else about Jesus?" he asked the centurion.

"Well, yes, I noticed something else that struck me with awe," answered the centurion. "When the soldiers came to Jesus to break his legs, as was the custom for a crucifixion, they didn't do it because he was already dead. Instead, one of the soldiers pierced Jesus' side with a spear, bringing a sudden flow of blood and water (John 19:33-34).

"The final thing that touched my heart," the centurion continued, "was when I saw a sheepskin on the ground, on which the mother of Jesus had been kneeling earlier in the day near the foot of the cross. That skin looked really old and worn. Its one corner already had some kind of deep red blemish on it. As the soldier's spear pierced Jesus' side and blood flowed forth, some of it spilled onto that sheepskin!"

On hearing this, Ethan burst into sobs and had to leave the scene because he felt as if his heart had been pierced, too. For days, Ethan wandered around the city, crushed with sorrow and hopelessness. Jesus, the one he first knew as the Christ child, the Son of God, was dead!

For about a week, Ethan heard rumors that Jesus had risen from his tomb and had been seen by the disciples more than once. Oh, if only he could see John so he could verify those rumors! Then, one day Ethan was with a group of about five hundred of Jesus' followers, when Jesus suddenly appeared to them (I Corinthians 15:3-6). Yes, He was alive! He had been raised from the dead! Ethan had to tell this great news to all with whom he came in contact.

* * *

Christ's Promise of the Holy Spirit
and
His Ascension

In his traveling about the area of Jerusalem to

spread the good news of Christ's Resurrection, Ethan occasionally saw John. About forty days after the resurrection, Ethan was thrilled when John told him that he and other disciples had seen Jesus taken up into heaven (Luke 24:-50-53). after telling them He would send the Holy Spirit to empower them, as He had promised. From the teachings of Jesus during the years He spent with the disciples, John assured Ethan this power was for all true followers of Jesus (John 14:16-17; 25-26; Luke 24:49a; Joel 2:28).

Ethan had one mission in life now, and that was to tell everyone about Jesus and how He died to save them from their sins and was in heaven preparing a place for those who believed on Him. Ethan had a special desire to tell the men who had served as shepherds with him, as all of them had gone throughout Bethlehem and the countryside on that night so long ago to tell of the birth of the Christ child.

Now, Ethan felt compelled to tell them how Jesus had died for their sins and rose again and was in heaven waiting for them. Truly, the one who had been the Christ Child was Jesus, the Son of God, the Savior!

Epilogue

A year or so had passed, and Ethan became restless. He couldn't determine if it was his need for adventure or if it were a true calling of God.

Once again, he seemed to be at a crossroads in his life. The aging Zebedee had moved in with one of his son's families. "Now what am I to do with my life?" Ethan questioned. (By that time Jesus had ascended into heaven, but He had sent His Spirit, the Holy Spirit, here on earth to guide the believer.) Ethan felt called by the Lord to serve Him somehow, but where or how? He would have to pray that the Holy Spirit would help him in his future search.

In one of his contacts with Jesus' disciples, James and John, Ethan learned of all the wonderful things the Holy Spirit had guided them to do in their ministry. Ethan listened with eager anticipation as the accounts stirred him spiritually–and in his adventuresome spirit.

However, his cousins also related some sad news. It was about Jesus' mother, Mary. Although still strong in her spirit, her body began showing the stress of what she had passed through during the past years. His cousins said Mary was still living in the village of Nazareth. Hearing that, Ethan determined in his heart that he wanted to go visit Mary as soon as possible.

She welcomed him graciously and shared all the accounts that had been relayed to her about the disciples of Jesus going hither and yon in spreading the Gospel. Mary felt Ethan must have the call of God on his life. Thus stating that fact, Ethan had a strong feeling that she was right! He wanted to reach the lost for Christ just as his cousins and other disciples were doing daily!

Then Mary shared with Ethan about the conversion

to faith of a man formerly called Saul of Tarsus, now called Paul. Her accounts were very similar to the other accounts he had overheard. His heart raced with excitement! In the back of his mind he thought: "What a privilege it would be to serve the Lord with Paul on those missionary trips!"

Mary saw Ethan was contemplating, so she quietly got up from where she was seated in order to give him time to hear from God concerning these matters. Then Mary went to a trunk in her home. There, she pulled out *The Sheepskin* that the shepherds had given to her on the night of Christ's birth. With trembling hands, she put it across Ethan's shoulders as a mantle. It was as though this was a confirmation from the Lord that, indeed, Ethan had received the call to go help Paul spread the Gospel.

"Even if I just go to serve Paul to meet his needs, I will also be serving Jesus!" he joyfully relayed to Mary.

He exclaimed, "To think God would match my need for adventure to His calling me to serve Him with Paul is beyond my wildest dreams!"

In the back of Ethan's mind he envisioned "the greatest adventure of my life—serving Jesus!"

* * *

If your heart is leading you to accept Christ as your Savior, pray to God as follows:

"Dear God, I know that I am a sinner. I want to turn from my sins, and I ask for your forgiveness. I believe that Jesus Christ is your Son. I believe that He died for my sins and that you raised Him to life. I want Him to come into my heart and to take control of my life. I want to trust Jesus as my Savior and follow Him as my Lord from this day forward. In Jesus' name, Amen."

May God bless you greatly in your new life! Go in peace.

About the Author

The late **MIRIAM TAYLOR WERT,** formerly of Port Royal PA–but who went to live with her daughter Sue near Hershey, PA–has written stories for magazines, as well as stories for publishers of children's take-home Sunday School papers. In 1996, at age 71, she wrote and had self-published her first full-length book about her beloved lifetime in Tuscarora Valley, Juniata County, Pennsylvania. The book was warmly received there, encouraging her to continue writing.

The Sheepskin (A Special Gift) was her first story of a fictional nature. Although the story concerning shepherds is fiction, it has a solid scriptural foundation of Bible references to carry through the truths of the rest of the story. This First Revision of it contains a number of additional chapters to what were in her manuscript originally.

Miriam and her late husband, C. Marlin Wert, observed their 70th wedding anniversary before his passing in 2014. They have two daughters, six grandchildren, and eight great-grandchildren.

Up until age 93, Miriam had the privilege of serving as one of the many online coaches to participants in the "Search for Jesus" (SFJ) Internet Bible Study Course offered free of charge by the Billy Graham Evangelistic Assn. (BGEA). Those interested in finding a personal discipleship coach may do so at the following web sites:

http://courses.goingfarther.net
http://cursos.yendomaslejos.net

With love,

to my

Mother,

Miriam

Taylor

Wert

-Sue

* * *

SWV Editor's note: The following relates how I was feeling six weeks after my Mother's death on December 18, 2019. On February 2, 2020 as I heard the strains of a Billy Graham Crusade re-run on television with Ethel Waters singing, "His Eye is on the Sparrow," I headed towards my computer when I heard the next number being sung: "Give Them All to Jesus . . . and He will turn your sorrow into JOY."

"Lord, I know you wanted me to begin listing my memories of Mom's affinity 'with the birds of the air,' and how she so enjoyed the variety of birds that You created. But it's too soon after losing her for me to begin to record herjourney . . . nevertheless, 'Not my will but Thine be done,' so I offer myself to do Your bidding as I begin my journey of recalling events—*memories of collaborations with Mother*–but where do I begin when the beginning is so far in the past?" –Sue

In Memory of Miriam Taylor Wert

One final collaboration--

The 'Someday Special' Quilt
by Susan Wert Vogt

From the time I was a teen, I collaborated on many projects with my Mother: sewing, composing music and lyrics, and writing in general, especially after I taught Mother how to use the computer when she retired in the mid-1980s when she was 61 years old.

Mother sensed from my childhood that I always loved bright colors, coloring books, embroidery, and sewing. Whenever Mom shared her thoughts with my sister Peggy and me about the variety of colors in this world, she always pointed out to us the colors of "the birds of the air." One of her favorite hymns at that time was Ethel Waters' signature song, "His Eye Is on the Sparrow," which didn't have brightly-colored feathers. But yet its variegated markings on the girth of its body and wings were an intrinsic work of art.

Throughout my early elementary years I loved to color, but then I reached a certain age and it was a common belief back then, "Big girls your age don't color," so I took up embroidery. I was obsessed with embroidering–a type of coloring for me–only using thread instead of crayons!

Mother knew how I loved to embroider so one

Christmas, when I was in my mid-teens, she mail-ordered a special gift for me—an embroidery pattern for a quilt. The reason it was so special was because Alaska and Hawaii became part of the United States that year, and the gift she gave me was an embroidery pattern for the now-fifty state birds of the USA. I don't remember any other gift Peggy or I got that Christmas, but I especially remember that one. Mother had touched my heartstrings with her gift of an embroidery quilt pattern for me. So as a teen, I began embroidering the quilt patches of individual birds representing each of the fifty states.

Back in the day, all adult beds were double beds, but I wanted a ten-inch border around the exterior of the quilt patches instead of the smaller size as shown on the quilt pattern, so I asked Mother first if she would mind if I enlarged the border. Mother's only comment was, "Why not? The quilt is yours to do with as you wish."

In the meantime, I also had taken up sewing, and I began to make my own dresses–just a big girl playing with (paper doll) dresses it seemed! I also made Mom's dresses while I was in high school (and throughout her lifetime). In fact, when she was President of the Tuscarora Valley School Board (the first woman on the board and its first president), she began to think "out loud" in my presence what she would wear that year when she handed me my high school diploma.

I took the hint, and together we collaborated, looking for maroon material which I fashioned into a two-piece summer-weight suit with an accompanying white blouse, since my school's colors were maroon and white. In that suit, Mother regally presented our class with our diplomas.

For my high school graduation, my Grandfather Charles H. Wert (who was also a bird lover) made me a cedar chest, and the pieced quilt top of embroidered birds was placed in it for "remembrance sake" of the two states added to the union, with the intention that the quilting would be completed at a later date. Eventually, the quilt of state birds was totally completed, but once again it was tucked away in my cedar chest "for someday special" or for "remembrance sake," or to "look back on the year Alaska and Hawaii were added to the union." Or so I thought.

Fast forward fifty-plus years. By then my beloved Dad had passed away in 2014 and my only sister (Peggy Love) passed in 2015, so Mother came to live with me, as I was widowed in 2016. At age 91, Mother looked forward to being with me, and I with her. After living with me over two years, Mother suffered two strokes within 60 days so that by December 18, 2018 it was necessary for her to go to a nursing home nearby. I visited with her almost every day, plus I called her on the phone each morning and again in the evening to "tuck her into bed" as I had done in my home.

One of the things that was the most troublesome for her at the nursing home was that her legs got cold.

The conventional nursing home blankets weren't wide enough to keep the air from flowing under her knees, which were elevated in order to lessen her back pain. I knew what I needed to do, and I knew then why I had been led to make my quilt wider than usual.

I went home and retrieved the bird quilt from my cedar chest; it was just the thing to lift Mother's spirits, plus its added width/length border kept her legs warm! She told me, "I feel your love all around me when I'm under this quilt!" My handiwork as a teen was to be saved for "someday special." It was; my Mother needed it and the love it represented to her as she aged.

Then, on December 17, 2019, I phoned Mom as usual after breakfast, and she answered and told me she was doing fine so I left my apartment to head for my dental appointment. I had just positioned myself in the dental chair when my cell phone rang; it was the nursing home. "We believe your Mother had a stroke, and we're taking her by ambulance to the hospital; meet us there," which I did. However, my Mother never got to talk with me again; she had suffered a brain-stem stroke and passed the following day.

When the time came for me to retrieve her things at the nursing home, to my chagrin the quilt was missing! No one seemed to know where it had disappeared!

Everything else of Mom's was accounted for, but not the quilt!

I took care of the necessary arrangements on behalf

of my Mother in the days following her death. A number of days passed when I got a phone call from the mortuary, informing me "Be sure to pick up the bag with a blanket and other belongings when you stop by later." It was then I discovered for what purpose the quilt had been used during Mother's final moments.

It was severely cold when Mother had been rushed to the hospital on December 17, 2019. In the rush, the attendants had no choice but to use the quilt in which to wrap Mom and put her in the pre-heated ambulance–there was no time even to put a coat over her or bundle her against the cold in any way–except with the quilt I had made. I hadn't realized that the quilt which she had used in the nursing home, also accompanied her to the hospital, and eventually to the mortuary.

In the weeks to follow, I got many sympathy cards, but one in particular stood out. It had four of Mother's favorite birds on it–a cardinal, a bluebird, a canary and a sparrow, which were also the most prevalent state birds on the quilt. Plus, that card signaled to me that I was to recall memories of my Mother via her love for "the fowls of the air."

In my memory, I heard my Mother's sweet voice singing, *"I sing because I'm happy; I sing because I'm free! His eye is on the sparrow, and I know He's watching me."*

Instead of a torrent of tears as I wrote this account, I experienced waves of comfort as I recalled past events. Many times the Lord has used something to indicate His care of me and my loved ones. In the above case, it was the recalling of the birds on a sympathy card and on the quilt I made that Mom had cherished.

This reminded me of a saying on one of the other sympathy cards sent to me which comforted me greatly: *"The one who rocked you in the beginning . . . needed you most in the end."* How true!

Not only was my presence with Mother via The 'Someday Special' Quilt she cherished, it served another purpose: The Lord Jesus used the quilt to comfort me that His orchestration and presence was in our lives as we collaborated together throughout the years as these memories flooded my mind:

Under the guidance of the Holy Spirit in 1959, my Mother had purchased a quilt pattern for me when I was a teen. That *"Someday Special' Quilt* had been pieced together *sixty years before* Mother's death. Its ultimate purpose would serve as a symbol of our one final collaboration together on earth, as my precious Mother was ushered into heaven.

Unknowingly we had always referred to it as "The 'Someday Special' Quilt." Little did we realize how special that day would be for Mother.

CPSIA information can be obtained
at www.ICGtesting.com
Printed in the USA
BVHW091938081220
595006BV00002B/8

9 781647 734046